MORN PRAYERS FOR KIDS 2024

A Fun and Meaningful Start to the Day

MARIA T. BLYTHE

Copyright © Maria T. Blythe

TABLE OF CONTENTS

INTRODUCTION

For kids, the morning is crucial because it sets the tone for the rest of the day. Morning prayers may be an effective strategy to inculcate values, improve mental health, and promote a good start to the day in children. In this session, we dig into the importance of morning prayers for children and look at methods for developing a positive daily habit.

Developing a Gratitude and Mindfulness Mindset

Children get the chance to show thanks during morning prayers. This straightforward action may foster gratitude for the positives in their life and encourage a more upbeat mindset. Children develop mindfulness, which may help with their general emotional development, when they repeat prayers or take time for introspection. Mindfulness helps children become more aware of their emotions and their environment.

Creating a Sense of Order and Discipline

Children's growth and development depend on routines. Including morning prayers in their daily schedule helps them develop structure and discipline. Children who continuously engage in this activity learn the value of dedication and timeliness, two traits that will benefit them throughout their lives.

Creating a Bond with Morals and Beliefs

One may connect with their principles and convictions via morning prayers. Children may consider the values that guide their lives through praying, whether they are religious or secular prayers. By strengthening their moral compass and giving them a feeling of purpose, this link might aid them in overcoming difficulties they may face during the day.

Building Emotional Wellbeing and Resilience

Even for young people, obstacles in life are common. Morning prayers may be a source of resiliency and power. Children are better prepared to confront challenges with optimism if they start the day with some introspection. A greater sense of general wellbeing may result from this emotional toughness.

Increasing Family Ties

Morning prayers may be a family affair that includes parents and children. This shared activity promotes community and fortifies ties among families. It offers a chance for open conversation and connecting, fostering a nurturing and caring atmosphere in which kids may flourish.

How to Establish a Positive Morning Routine

Parents and other adults who are responsible for children may implement morning prayers into a child's routine by doing the following:

1. Pick a Regular Time: To create a habit, pick a set time each morning for prayers.

2. Establish a Warm Environment: Set aside a quiet, distraction-free space for prayer.

3. Use Age-Appropriate Material: Choose meditations or prayers that are appropriate for the child's age and level of understanding.

4. Promote Participation: Involve kids in choosing or writing their prayers to personalize the ritual.

5. Set a Good Example: Parents and other adults who provide care for children should take part as well.

6. Discuss Values: After prayers, spend some time talking about the morals and teachings that were emphasized.

7. Practice Gratitude: Practice being appreciative by asking kids to share one item they are grateful for every morning.

Children may gain a lot from morning prayers, including the development of awareness and thankfulness as well as the reinforcement of morals and resilience. These habits set the groundwork for a constructive and intentional start to each day, encouraging emotional wellbeing and enhancing family ties when paired with a well-organized morning routine.

CHAPTER 1

Understanding Prayer

We set out on a quest to comprehend the deep idea of prayer itself in the first chapter of our investigation into the realm of prayer. This fundamental component of several cultures and faiths acts as a link between the material and the spiritual, providing consolation, direction, and a channel for interceding with a higher force. But when teaching prayer to children, what precisely is it?

What Is Prayer? Explained for Kids

My dear young minds, prayer is like having a one-on-one conversation with the universe or a higher force. It's a way of expressing your ideas, feelings, hopes, and goals, whether it's spoken aloud or silently in your brain. Consider it as a way to talk to someone who is always listening, even when no one else is there.

Let's now clarify it a little more:

1. Talking to the Define: Prayer is frequently about communicating with a higher power, such as God, the universe, or whatever you believe in. It's like sending a message to a strong buddy who is willing to support, mentor, or simply listen.

2. Expressing Emotions: Prayer may also be an opportunity to voice your emotions. You may give thanks to the divine while you're joyful. You can ask for solace and bravery when you're feeling depressed or afraid.

3. Making Requests: It's OK to include requests in your prayers. Perhaps you need assistance with an issue or have a unique request. Your opportunity to express these wishes is prayer.

Many Types of Prayer

There are many distinct ways to pray, and they vary between cultures and religions:

1. Meditative Prayer: Some people discover calm via silent meditation, focusing their minds, and making a profound, thoughtful connection with God.

2. Customary Prayers: The Lord's Prayer in Christianity and the Salat in Islam are two examples of traditional prayers. These prayers follow certain routines and language.

3. Spontaneous Prayer: You are free to speak your own prayers at anytime, anyplace. This is the time for heart-to-heart communication with the divine.

4. Prayer Beads and Rituals: To improve their prayer experience, several cultures employ objects like prayer beads or certain stances and gestures.

5. Silence and Nature: For some people, seeking periods of silence or being in nature is a type of prayer, a means to commune with the divine through the beauty of the earth.

A beautiful and varied activity, prayer enables individuals to communicate with the divine, express their emotions, and ask for things. Depending on your beliefs and interests, it can take on a variety of forms and function much like a dialogue with a higher power. The ability to comprehend prayer opens up a world of spiritual connection and self-discovery.

CHAPTER 2

The Power of Gratitude

A child's life can be significantly improved by the transformational feeling of gratitude. In this chapter, we examine the tremendous effects of appreciation on children and offer methods for instilling thankfulness in them. In order to start the day off well, we also provide enjoyable appreciation activities that may be included into morning rituals.

The Transformative Power of Gratitude: Gratitude is a powerful feeling that may alter a child's perception of the world. It is not merely a polite statement. Children who comprehend and practice thankfulness have numerous important advantages:

Enhanced Emotional Well-Being: Encouraging children to notice and value the good things in their lives can boost their happiness and lower their stress levels. Children who are thankful are more prone to concentrate on their gifts than to linger on their shortcomings.

Improved Relationships: Relationships are improved because gratitude encourages kindness and empathy. Children who express gratitude are more likely to show empathy and consideration for others, which improves their connections with their classmates, family, and friends.

Resilience in Adversity: Gratitude gives kids a sense of perspective, which fosters resilience in the face of adversity. Children who are appreciative are more likely to see the bright side of situations and keep a positive outlook, which strengthens their resilience in the face of difficulty.

Physical condition: According to research, those who are appreciative tend to be in better physical condition. By easing stress and encouraging good habits, teaching kid's gratitude can improve their general well-being.

Teaching Children Gratitude

Gratitude is an important life trait that may be instilled in kids using the following methods:

Show Gratitude To Others: Kids observe what adults do. Regularly and out loudly express your personal thankfulness, whether it is for a stunning sunset, a hearty dinner, or a kind act.

Encourage Daily Reflection: Establish a daily practice that invites children to consider the things for which they are thankful. They can share their "gratitude moments" for the day at meals or before going to bed.

Teach Perspective: By assisting kids in realizing that not everyone enjoys the same advantages and blessings. Encourage them to consider others who are less fortunate and how they may improve someone else's life.

Express Appreciation: Encourage kids to vocally or physically show their appreciation by performing small deeds of kindness. For people they appreciate, drawing images or writing thank-you cards can be thoughtful ways to express their gratitude.

Morning Gratitude Activities That Are Fun

Children may learn about thankfulness during their morning activities. These enjoyable activities might make the day feel more optimistic:

Gratitude Jar: Make a "gratitude jar" and set it out on the breakfast table. Family members can write something they're thankful for on a piece of paper and place it in the jar every morning. When the family is together, read the notes aloud.

Gratitude Circle: Form a circle as a family and participate in the gratitude exercise. Share one item you are thankful for this morning in turn. Simple things like the sun or a restful night's sleep may do it.

Gratitude Journal: Give kids gratitude diaries so they may record or illustrate things they are grateful for every morning. To demonstrate their thankfulness in a unique way, exhort them.

Gratitude Art: Set up an art station with materials like colored pencils, markers, and paper for gratitude art. Encourage kids to make art that expresses what they are thankful for. As a reminder of the beauty in their life, display their creations.

We've spoken about the importance of teaching kids to feel thankfulness as well as how it may change your life. Parents and other caregivers may cultivate a spirit of appreciation in children that will serve them well throughout their lives by including enjoyable gratitude activities into their morning routines.

CHAPTER 3

Morning Prayer Rituals

As we continue to read this book about children's spiritual development, Chapter 3 sheds light on the importance of Morning Prayer customs. By praying in the morning, you may give your day optimism, concentration, and a sense of being part of something bigger. Making this daily practice a meaningful and fulfilling part of your life, we'll look at how to set up a designated prayer place and choose the best time for morning prayers in this chapter.

Creating a Prayer Room

You might establish a bridge to the divine by designating a specific location for your morning prayers. Here's how to create a personalized prayer place for yourself:

1. Select a peaceful space: Look for a peaceful space in your room or other home location where you won't be bothered. You are better able to focus in a calm setting.

2. Mindfully decorate: Include stuff that motivates you. It may be a tiny shrine with a candle, some new flowers, or a picture or symbol of your religion. You may be reminded of the holiness of your area by these objects.

3. Comfort is Key: Ensure that you are at ease. To sit on, you could choose a plush cushion or a prayer mat. Relaxation makes it easier to concentrate on your prayers.

4. Eliminate Distractions: Keep any toys, technology, and other items out of your meditation space. This unique connection time is between you.

The Best Time to Say Your Morning Prayers

The time you pray in the morning can have a significant impact on how you begin your day. Here are some things to think about:

1. Dawn: Many cultures and faiths advise prayer in the early hours of the morning, when everything is still and a new day is just beginning. It's a metaphor for a new beginning.

2. Sunrise: If you get up early, you could enjoy praying as the sun rises. It serves as a reminder of the grandeur and beauty of nature.

3. Before Breakfast: For kids, praying before breakfast might be useful. By doing this, you may begin each day with thanksgiving and good intentions.

4. After Morning Routine: After brushing their teeth and getting ready for the day, some kids like to pray. It serves as a bridge between the ordinary and the sacred.

5. Family Time: If your family practices family prayer, work with them to determine a time that is convenient for everyone. This shared experience can strengthen relationships.

Always keep in mind that you should pray in the morning at whatever hour seems comfortable to you. It's a question of personal preference, and what counts most is the sincerity and commitment you bring to your daily prayers. You may begin each day with a sense of serenity and purpose in your prayer place at the time of your choosing, establishing a good tone for the experiences that are ahead.

CHAPTER 4

Kid-Friendly Prayers

We examine the value of kid-friendly prayers as we continue on our exploration of the realm of children's spirituality. These prayers are created with young minds in mind, making them approachable, relevant, and interesting, fostering a strong bond with their religion and a sense of spiritual well-being. To make sure that prayer is a meaningful and pleasant part of their life, we'll dig into straightforward prayers appropriate for young children as well as more engaging prayers designed for older kids.

Simple Invocations for Children

Simplicity is essential for the younger members of our spiritual group. These straightforward prayers are simple to memories and comprehend:

1. Thank You, Universe: Foster thankfulness by asking the universe to be thanked for the day, their loved ones, and the food they consume. It aids in the formation of the habit of appreciation in children.

2. Now I Lay Me Down to Sleep: This traditional nighttime chant helps reassure and calm you before you go to sleep.

3. Bless Our Family: A brief prayer that asks for blessings and protection for family members helps people feel more connected and in love.

4. Mealtime Gratitude: Teaching children to express gratitude at mealtimes by having them recite a brief "thank you" prayer in order to express gratitude for the food and those who prepared it.

5. Help Me Be Nice: Promote kindness by requesting assistance in being nice to people, animals, and the environment.

Prayers that Involve Older Children

Growing up, children get a deeper knowledge and may value more interesting prayers:

1. The Serenity Prayer: Instill in older children the knowledge of knowing the difference between accepting what they cannot change and having the fortitude to change it

2. Compassionate Prayer: Encourage empathy and a feeling of social duty by directing children to pray for those who are in need.

3. Gratitude Journal Prayer: Incorporate writing and prayer by having children list or express three things they are grateful for each day. This encourages optimism and awareness.

4. Prayer for Strength: Teach them a prayer to help them discover inner strength when faced with difficulties, which will help them develop resilience.

5. Prayer for Guidance: Encourage older children to pray for help when they are faced with problems or conundrums. They may grow to trust their faith and intuition as a result of this.

These kid-friendly prayers provide the groundwork for long-term spiritual development. These prayers, whether straightforward or complex, offer solace, impart morals, and give kids a platform to express their feelings. Kids may connect with their beliefs and find comfort in prayer in the holy environment they help to build.

CHAPTER 5

Creative Prayer Activities

Let's go into the world of imaginative prayer activities as we continue our investigation into Morning Prayer for children. Praying with young people may be a fun and rewarding experience. We shall examine how narrative, art and craft, and nature can all be effective teaching methods for kids to develop their spirituality and develop a love of morning prayers.

Prayers Involving the Arts

Kids have a great outlet for expressing their emotions and ideas via visual creativity thanks to art and craft. Fun and spiritually gratifying activities can be incorporated into Morning Prayer:

1. Prayer Collages: Encourage kids to make prayer collages by giving them images or words to use as symbols for their prayers or things they are grateful for. They are able to graphically communicate their ideas through this practical practice.

2. Prayer Pebbles: Small pebbles can be painted with motivational phrases or symbols to act as physical reminders of one's prayers. These rocks can be kept by children in their prayer corner or given to loved ones.

3. Prayer Flags: Children may make their own flags with vibrant patterns and prayers written on them, just like the traditional Tibetan prayer flags. These flags hanging there give the area where they pray a colorful touch.

4. Prayer Mandalas: Making or coloring mandalas can help people focus their thoughts during prayer in a contemplative and artistic way. Different facets of their prayer can be represented by each area of the mandala.

Narrative Prayers

Children can be drawn into prayer via storytelling, which also helps them relate to spiritual ideas:

1. Bible Tales: Sharing Bible tales as a family may be a wonderful method for Christian families to strengthen their faith. Children can give prayers in connection with the narrative and discuss the moral teachings after reading.

2. Personal Narratives: Inspire children to share their own tales of thankfulness or instances in which they sensed the divine's influence in their life. These tales might inspire sincere thanksgiving prayers.

3. Imaginative Tales: Encourage kids to write their own short stories that share morals of compassion, love, and faith to let their imaginations run wild. These tales may substitute for their morning prayers.

Prayers Inspired by Nature

A sense of wonder and spirituality may be fostered through connecting with nature. Use these exercises to include nature into your morning prayers:

1. Outdoor Prayers: Take your morning prayers outside, whether it's in a garden, park, or your backyard. Encourage children to appreciate and observe the beauty of nature.

2. Nature Journaling: Give children diaries to record their experiences with nature. They can doodle, compose poetry, or just scribble down their ideas and requests that are motivated by the natural environment.

3. Prayer Walks: Take kids on brief prayer walks so they may contemplate nature's marvels in silence. This peaceful interaction with the natural world may be a profoundly spiritual one.

Kids' morning prayers are made more joyful through imaginative prayer activities, which also help them grasp spirituality better. Children may establish a deep connection with their religion and the world around them via art, storytelling, and nature, establishing a good tone for the rest of the day.

CHAPTER 6

Prayers for Different Occasions

We will explore the realm of morning prayers created especially for children. Morning prayers are a great way to start the day off right since they encourage awareness, appreciation, and a relationship with God. We'll look at the morning prayers for school days and the morning prayers for weekends and holidays.

Morning Meditations for Academic Days

It's time to get ready for another day of growth and learning as the sun begins to rise. Children can start their school days off on the right foot by saying their morning prayers. In these prayers, children frequently ask for protection, wisdom, and direction as they enter the outside world. They act as a reminder of the worth of traits like compassion, tolerance, and tenacity.

Gratitude is a prominent subject in these prayers. Children are encouraged to show gratitude for the chance to learn and develop, for their instructors' inspiration and guidance, and for their classmates' contribution to the fun of the trip. These prayers frequently ask for bravery and strength to confront difficulties and to be an inspiration to their school's community.

Holiday and Weekend Prayers

Weekends and holidays provide an opportunity for relaxation, entertainment, and quality family time by offering a break from the monotony of school. Children learn the value of relaxation and the joy of leisure via these morning prayers. These prayers frequently center on concepts of community, thanksgiving for time spent with loved ones, and the beauty of the earth.

The marvels of nature and the everyday joys of living are taught to children. They could show appreciation for the chance to engage in extracurricular activities like play and learning. These prayers frequently include aspects of mindfulness, which supports children in remaining in the present and appreciating their free time.

Kids may be encouraged to include thoughts of people who are less fortunate and methods to share their blessings with others throughout the weekends and during holidays in these prayers. These prayers cultivate in kids a sense of empathy and compassion, whether it is via deeds of kindness or spending time with individuals who might be lonely.

Whether on school days, weekends, or holidays, morning prayers for children are a source of motivation, wisdom, and thankfulness. They encourage ideals that will serve children well throughout their life and help them start the day with a cheerful outlook. These prayers provide kids a chance to pause and connect while also being reminded of the world's beauty and the value of having compassion for others. Through these regular practices, children are not only spiritually enlightened but also equipped to meet the joys and difficulties of each day with a positive outlook.

CHAPTER 7

Praying with the Family

Let's talk about the importance of morning prayers for children in relation to family life. Family prayer time is a valued custom in many homes, providing children with a meaningful opportunity to interact with their loved ones and foster their spiritual development. We will discuss the significance of fostering family prayer time as well as the custom of discussing one's own joys and worries at these revered times.

Promotion of Family Prayer Time

A common practice in many homes is family prayer time, during which parents and kids meet to begin the day in a spirit of harmony and dedication. This practice promotes a feeling of community, teaches kids the importance of faith, and creates a secure environment for honest dialogue.

The family's morning prayers emphasize the value of meditation and thankfulness, setting a good tone for the day. Children learn through observation, so when they witness their parents and siblings praying, they are more likely to adopt this practice as a lifetime routine. By fostering moral and ethical ideals, family prayer time furthers the notion that religion and spirituality are integral parts of family life.

Parents can opt to say conventional prayers or let kids use their own language to convey their sentiments during these prayers. Kids may interact with spirituality in a way that resonates with them thanks to this versatility. It's a moment when kids may connect with the divine with their families and feel heard and appreciated.

Sharing Individual Concerns and Joys

The chance to communicate individual joys and concerns during family prayer time is one of its most lovely features. This approach promotes emotional intelligence and empathy in children by encouraging them to be open and honest about their feelings. Parents may teach their children to show thankfulness for the good things in their life, such as accomplishments, joyous occasions, and family love.

Children can express their anxieties, fears, and concerns in a secure environment during family prayer. It's an opportunity for parents to reassure and encourage their children as they negotiate hurdles and challenging emotions. The concept that prayer is not just about asking for supernatural aid but also about finding support and solace within the family unit is reinforced by this practice.

The relationships between family members are strengthened when personal joys and worries are included in family prayer time. Everyone is able to connect on a deeper level as a result, sharing in each other's happiness and anxiety as well as providing emotional support.

We've talked about the benefits of family prayer time for kids, highlighting how it fosters a sense of community, instills spiritual values, and provides a forum for open dialogue. Parents enhance emotional wellbeing and improve family ties by enabling kids to express their unique joys and worries at these holy occasions. In the end, saying morning prayers as a family develops into a treasured custom that influences kids' relationships and values for the rest of their lives.

CHAPTER 8

Morning Meditation and Mindfulness

The morning is the perfect time to introduce kids to the practices of meditation and mindfulness since the day's beginning sets the tone for all that comes after. Find a calm, cozy area for your youngster to sit or lie down as a starting point. Encourage them to take a few deep breaths and to close their eyes. They are able to connect with their inner selves during this quiet time, which promotes emotional stability and self-awareness.

Children's Breathing Exercises

Giving children breathing exercises to practice may be a fun and rewarding method to improve their morning prayers. The exercise "bunny breaths" is one example. Have your kid pretend that they are a rabbit and instruct them to breathe slowly and deeply through their nose (the bunny sniffing) and then softly out of their lips (the bunny blowing out a candle). This enjoyable activity increases the link between the mind and body while also calming the mind.

The "flower breath" is an excellent breathing practice. Ask your youngster to visualize holding a lovely flower. They should take a big breath in through their nose and pretend to smell the blossom while they do so. They can blow on the fictitious flower with their exhalation to aid in its blossoming. This activity promotes mindfulness of the present moment and thankfulness.

Morning Prayers with Mindfulness

The spiritual connection and comprehension of a youngster can be strengthened by including mindfulness into morning prayers. Explain the significance of each prayer or scripture to them at first, urging them to think about it. Encourage your kid to concentrate on the words of the prayer, concentrating on their meaning and goal.

For instance, you may stress the phrase *"Give us this day our daily bread"* from the Lord's Prayer by talking about how important it is to be grateful for the benefits we get each day. Encourage your youngster to consider the people and things in their lives for which they are grateful. This kind of prayer that emphasizes mindfulness cultivates gratitude and awareness.

Kids' morning prayers are more than just recitations of verses; they provide them a chance to practice mindfulness, thankfulness, and inner calm. We can help kids start their days with a stronger connection to themselves and their faith by introducing morning meditation, involving breathing exercises, and promoting attentive moments during prayers.

CHAPTER 9

Overcoming Morning Challenges

A lovely tradition that creates a good outlook for the day. Like any regimen, it might occasionally provide its own set of difficulties. We are going to look at strategies for helping kids get through typical morning challenges including controlling morning grumpiness and managing morning tension and worry.

How to Manage Morning Grumpiness

Like adults, kids sometimes wake up on the wrong side of the bed, cranky or angry. It's crucial to handle these emotions with kindness. One strategy is to start a daily habit of thankfulness. Encourage your youngster to consider one item for which they are grateful before beginning their prayers. This straightforward exercise can help them change their attention from grumbling to expressing gratitude, which will help their morning prayers go more smoothly.

Making a morning routine that includes delightful activities is another useful tactic. These little pleasures, whether they involve playing a brief game, enjoying a favorite meal, or spending some time together reading a fun book, can help ease morning grouchiness and make prayer time more pleasurable.

Managing Morning Anxiety and Stress

Children may experience morning tension and anxiety for a variety of reasons, including impending examinations, social anxiety, or even a fear of the unknown. Consider including relaxation exercises in their Morning Prayer ritual to help with these emotions.

The "Worry Jar" is one such tactic. Before saying the morning prayers, have your kid put any tension or anxiety they may be experiencing on a little piece of paper and put it in a jar. Tell children that they may put their worries in this jar safely and come back to them if necessary. In doing so, kids are able to let go of tension and concentrate during prayer.

Conducting a brief mindfulness practice with your child is another beneficial tactic. Ask them to close their eyes, take a few deep breaths, and picture a serene setting.

Encourage them to employ this visualization throughout their morning ritual anytime they experience tension or anxiety.

Utilizing these strategies teaches kids important life lessons about controlling emotions and finding serenity despite everyday tensions in addition to help them deal with morning issues. Setting a good tone for the day, Morning Prayer might turn into a haven of solace and resiliency for them.

CHAPTER 10

Celebrating Milestones and Achievements

This chapter holds a special place in the realm of Morning Prayers for children. It is this chapter that teaches kids to value and express gratitude for their accomplishments. It serves as a reminder that thankfulness should permeate all aspects of life and is not only something to be saved for the biggest victories.

Special Blessings for Birthdays and Success

Birthdays are among the most special occasions in a child's life. It's a day of celebration, cake, and gifts, but it's also a chance to foster a spirit of thanksgiving. Children can learn to say a particular prayer for the gift of another year of life, for the love of family and friends gathered together, and for the adventures that wait for them, rather than merely concentrating on the presents they have received.

No matter how great or little, accomplishments need to be acknowledged. A special prayer may be a lovely way to recognize the work and celebrate the achievement when a kid succeeds at something—whether it's doing well on a test, winning a sporting event, or achieving a personal goal. These prayers show children that their accomplishments are not just about their own glory, but also about the effort and help they received to get there.

Considering Personal Development

This chapter's morning prayers also exhort children to consider their personal development. They are actively considering how they have changed and developed; they are not merely repeating phrases. This self-examination might serve as inspiration for them as they make new resolutions and work to improve them.

Children can learn to be particular while thanking someone rather than just stating, "Thank you for this day." Expressions of appreciation that encourage reflection and development include, "Thank you for helping me become a better friend," or "Thank you for guiding me through difficulties that made me stronger."

Kids are urged to take a minute during their morning prayers to enjoy the path of life and the individual milestones along the way. They are reminded in this chapter that each day is a gift, every accomplishment is deserving of praise, and every step toward personal development is important. Children may take these qualities with them throughout their lives, enhancing their spiritual and emotional wellbeing, by encouraging thankfulness and introspection in their daily prayers.

CHAPTER 11

Cultivating Values through Morning Prayers

Children's morning prayers are extremely important for developing their moral character and establishing fundamental values. This chapter will examine how morning prayers, with a particular emphasis on kindness and compassion, are a powerful instrument for developing values. We will also explore the relevance of utilizing tales and parables to teach students important truths about life.

Fostering Values like Compassion and Benevolence

Morning prayers are more than simply rituals; they are an opportunity to teach kids morals. Kindness is one of the most essential virtues we can instill in children. Children can learn to be nice to themselves as well as others via daily prayers. Children are taught the value of looking out for the wellbeing of others by showing thankfulness for the day ahead and praying for blessings for loved ones.

Morning prayers can foster compassion, another important characteristic. Children may develop a compassionate heart by being taught to pray for the poor, to understand the hardships of others, and to ask for advice when it comes to assisting the less fortunate. Children can connect with the larger world and develop a sense of responsibility for it via morning prayers.

Learning through Parables and Stories

Morning prayers may successfully employ the power of storytelling to communicate ideals since stories and parables have been used for millennia to teach moral teachings. Parents and teachers might use short tales or parables that correspond with the ideals they want to promote rather than just repeating prayers.

For instance, a prayer emphasizing the value of kindness may be spoken after a tale of a good-hearted youngster who helps a fellow student in need. The ideals are made more apparent and approachable for kids via the use of these stories as real-world illustrations.

Children can have a deeper grasp of various values and viewpoints by using parables from many cultures and faiths. This exposure promotes respect, tolerance, and a more open-minded perspective on the world.

We have discussed the usefulness of morning prayers in developing moral principles, with an emphasis on kindness and compassion. We can make learning more interesting and meaningful for kids by including tales and parables into these prayers. We have the chance to shape the character of the future generation and encourage them to lead compassionate, caring, and socially responsible lives via this everyday practice.

CHAPTER 12

Building a Lifelong Habit

Children's morning prayers can have a significant influence on both their immediate well-being and their long-term spiritual and emotional growth. In this chapter, we'll look at ways to help kids develop the habit of saying their prayers in the morning and how to help them carry that habit throughout adolescence and adulthood.

Forming a Routine of Morning Prayers

It is important to help kids develop the everyday practice of saying their prayers in the morning. As habits are frequently carried over into adulthood, developing a prayer pattern can have long-lasting advantages. Here are some methods for developing the practice of morning prayers:

1. Consistency: Establish a regular prayer time each morning, whether it's directly when you wake up, before breakfast, or before you go for school. Children learn the importance of morning prayers as a part of their daily routine via consistency.

2. Engagement: Create a fun and interesting Morning Prayer experience. Use prayers that are appropriate for children's ages and incorporate appealing aspects like music, kid-friendly tales, or time for introspection.

3. Parental Involvement: Parents are extremely important in fostering this behavior. Join your child in morning prayers and show them the importance of them by participating yourself.

4. Visual Aids: To designate an area for morning prayers, use visual aids like a prayer nook or a tiny altar. Children may remember and look forward to this everyday activity with the aid of this visual reminder.

5. Encouragement: Applaud and support your youngster for his or her dedication to morning prayers. They may be inspired to keep up this practice by receiving positive reinforcement.

Developing Teen and Adult Prayer Habits

Their prayer habits should change as kids develop into teens, then into adults, to reflect their evolving needs and comprehension. Here's how to make the shift go smoothly:

1. Open Communication: Keep the lines of communication with your child concerning their spiritual development open. Encourage them to ponder their views and raise questions. This could result in more distinctive praying habits.

2. Autonomy: Give teens the freedom to choose their own prayer practices. They could decide to investigate various mindfulness practices, meditation techniques, or even religious traditions. Respect their decisions while advising them.

3. Flexibility: Take into account the fact that everyone has a different approach to prayer. Encourage adaptability and tolerance for various spiritual practices

4. Ongoing Encouragement: Continue to encourage and mentor kids as they grow into adults. Share your personal wisdom with them while letting them decide on their own spiritual practices.

For children, creating a daily routine of morning prayers is important. To ensure that this habit persists, consistency, engagement, and parental participation are essential. Maintaining open communication and flexibility will assist guarantee that children have a meaningful and lasting relationship to spirituality throughout their lives. As children mature, their prayer practices should change to meet their evolving needs.

CONCLUSION

Children's morning prayers provide a variety of long-lasting advantages and are a crucial part of fostering a spiritual path in kids. This chapter has examined the practice's enduring benefits and emphasized how it fosters a child's spiritual and emotional growth.

The Long-Term Advantages of Morning Prayers

Children learn discipline and routine through morning prayers, building a solid foundation for lasting behaviors. This approach has advantages that go well beyond young children:

1. Emotional Resilience: Children who participate in morning prayers experience inner serenity and emotional resilience. It helps people approach issues with a more balanced perspective to begin the day with appreciation and good intentions.

2. Morals and values: Children acquire significant morals via their daily prayers, including kindness, compassion, thankfulness, and empathy. Throughout their life, these principles mound their personality and direct how they interact with others.

3. Connection to Spirituality: Children are introduced to spirituality and the idea of a higher power via the practice of morning prayers. As they develop, this foundation may pave the way for a more profound and fulfilling spiritual experience.

4. Family Bonding: Morning prayers frequently include family members, fostering a particular moment of family unity. These shared experiences can foster close familial ties that last well into adulthood.

5. Healthy Habits: Making morning prayers a habit early in life increases the probability that one will continue spiritual activities as they mature. It may also encourage a greater dedication to personal development and self-care.

Children's morning prayers are a potent instrument for creating a solid, lifelong foundation of morals, emotional fortitude, and spirituality. By fostering this practice and encouraging your child's unique spiritual path, you provide them the tools they need to live a life filled with meaning, compassion, and a stronger sense of connectedness to the world.

Printed in Great Britain
by Amazon